FIFE COUNCIL LIBRARIES
FC912181

KT-555-5

Clothes Around the World

Uniforms and Work Clothes

Jane Bingham

WAYLAND

First published in 2008 by Wayland

Wayland
Hachette Children's Books
338 Euston Road
London NW1 3BH

Wayland
Level 17/207 Kent Street
Sydney NSW 2000

Senior editor: Joyce Bentley
Design: Holly Fullbrook and Rachel Hamdi
Picture researcher: Kathy Lockley

British Library in Cataloguing in Publication Data
Bingham, Jane
Uniforms and work clothes. - (Clothes around the world)
1. Uniforms - Juvenile literature
2. Work clothes - Juvenile literature
I. Title
391

ISBN 978 0 7502 5314 7

Picture acknowledgements: Pete Atkinson/Stone/Getty Images: 22; Graham Bell/Corbis: 12; Construction Photography/Corbis: 14; Robert Essel NYC/Corbis: 24 Owen Franken/Corbis: 16; Bertrand Gardel/Hemis/Corbis: 6; Getty Images: 20; Mike Goldwater/Alamy: 25; Jeff Greenberg/Alamy: 20; image100/Corbis: 17; Wilfried Krecichwost/zefa/Corbis: 19; Frank Lukasseck/Corbis: 8; Jenny Matthews/Alamy: 5; NASA-KSC: 23; Oxford Event Photography/Alamy: 26 Frederic Pitchal/Sygma/Corbis: 4; Private Collection/©John Noott Galleries, Broadway, Worcestershire, UK: 10; Bob Sacha/Corbis: 15; Steve Skjold/Alamy: 7; Michael St Maur Sheil/Corbis: 9; Vince Steano/Corbis: 1, 27; Bill Stormont/Corbis: 18; Thinkstock/Corbis: 13; Peter M. Wilson/Alamy: 3, 1; Wishlist: 28-30

Printed in China

Wayland is a division of Hachette Children's Books,
an Hachette Livre UK company.

Contents

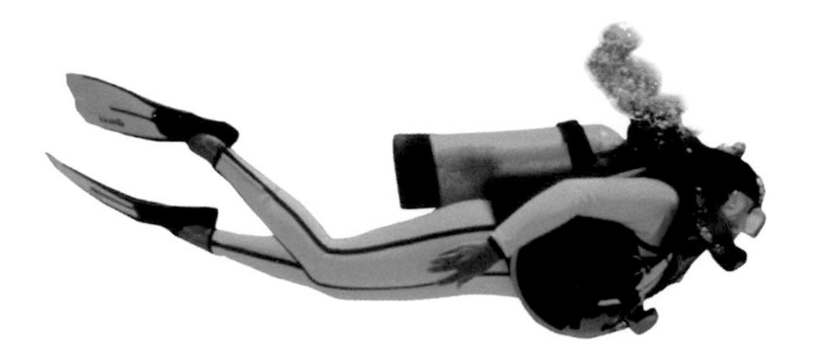

Why do people wear uniforms and work clothes?

People often wear special clothes for work. They may wear a uniform, or they may have some other kind of workwear. Most work clothes are hardwearing and comfortable. They are specially designed to be easy to work in.

It Works!

Useful coveralls

Many people wear loose cotton coveralls for work. Coveralls are made of strong material with lots of pockets to keep things in. They protect your clothes and are easy to wear. You can wear as much or as little as you like underneath them, so you don't get too hot or too cold.

Wearing a uniform makes you stand out. Uniforms can show what job you do, what school you go to, or what **organization** you belong to.

Some special workwear can help to keep you safe at work. Wearing the right workwear can also help you do a better job.

Uniforms and work clothes make you look neat, tidy and smart. They can make you feel proud of yourself and the job you do.

Many schools have their own uniform. Do you wear a school uniform?

Uniforms and workwear around the world

People around the world wear different kinds of workwear. Their work clothes are suited to the jobs they do, and to the weather in their country.

In Thailand, farmers work in flooded rice fields. They wear a cotton shirt with a sarong. Sarongs are made from a strip of cloth, tucked in at the waist to form a kind of skirt. They are cool and easy to wear if people are working in muddy rice fields.

A rice farmer works in a cotton sarong and shirt. The wide straw hat keeps the sun off the farmer's face.

When the **Inuit** people go hunting on the ice, they wear padded clothes that are usually lined with fur. These warm, thick clothes protect people from the cold. The padding cushions their bodies if they fall.

It Works!

Mexican workwear

In the mountains of Mexico, cattle herders wear a poncho – a kind of thick blanket with a hole for the head. The herders stay very warm in their ponchos, but their arms and hands are left completely free. At night, the herders wrap themselves in their ponchos before they go to sleep.

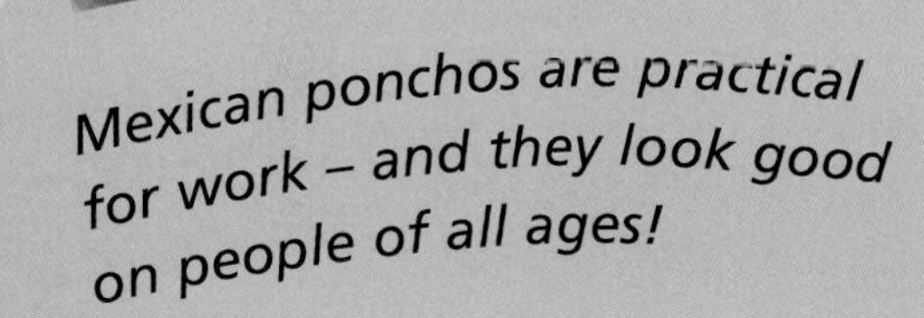

Mexican ponchos are practical for work – and they look good on people of all ages!

The history of uniforms and workwear

Soldiers have been wearing uniforms for thousands of years. One of the earliest armies came from China. Chinese soldiers wore leather tunics with metal studs. They also wore cotton caps on their heads. Soldiers of different ranks wore different styles of cap.

Roman soldiers dressed in short tunics and sandals. In battle they wore a helmet and a metal breastplate. Each rank had a different helmet. The army's commander wore a helmet with golden wings.

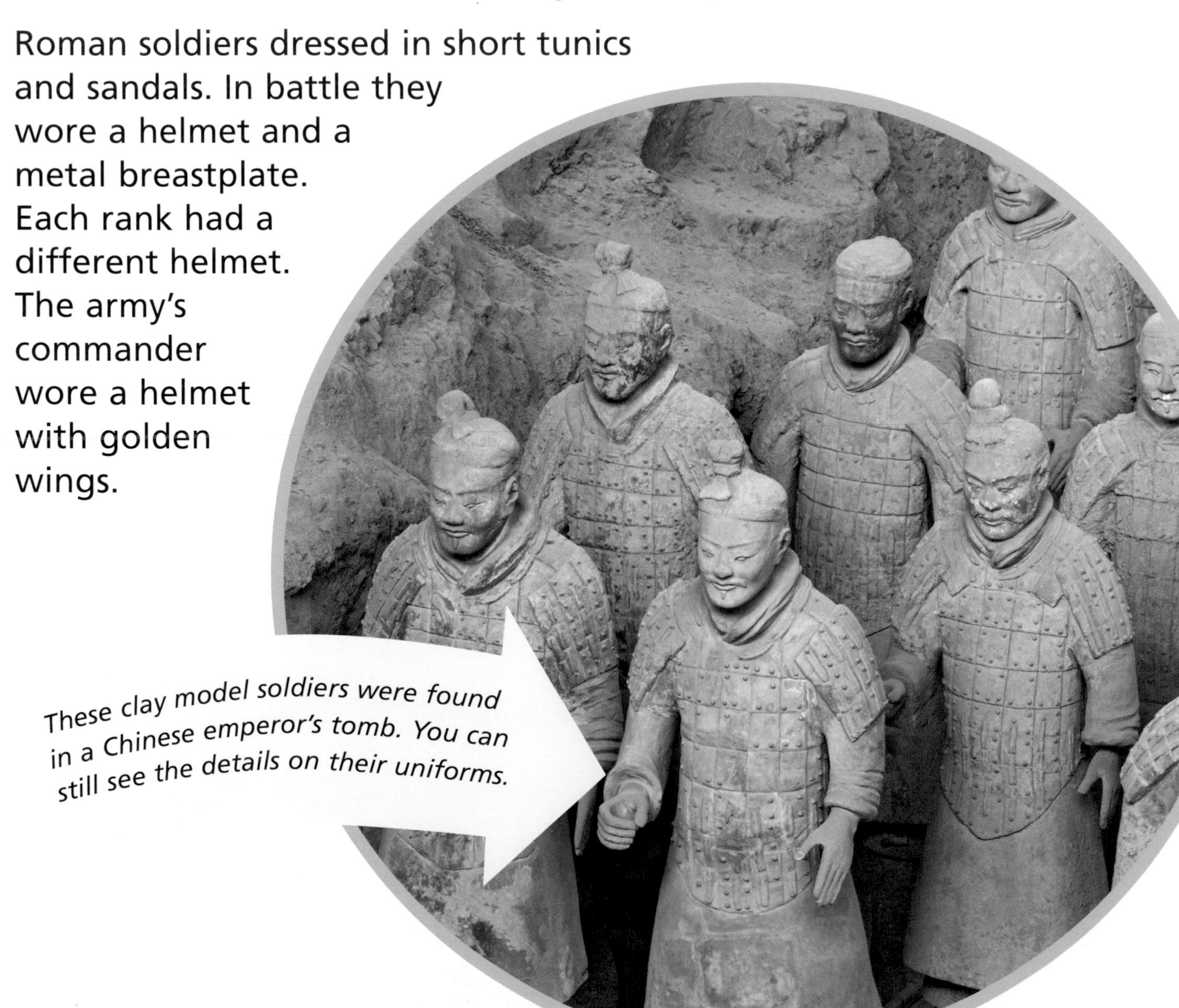

These clay model soldiers were found in a Chinese emperor's tomb. You can still see the details on their uniforms.

In **medieval times,** knights wore suits of armour that covered their body completely. The suits were made from many sheets of metal, fixed together with pins. The armour had hinges at the elbows and knees so the knights could move a little.

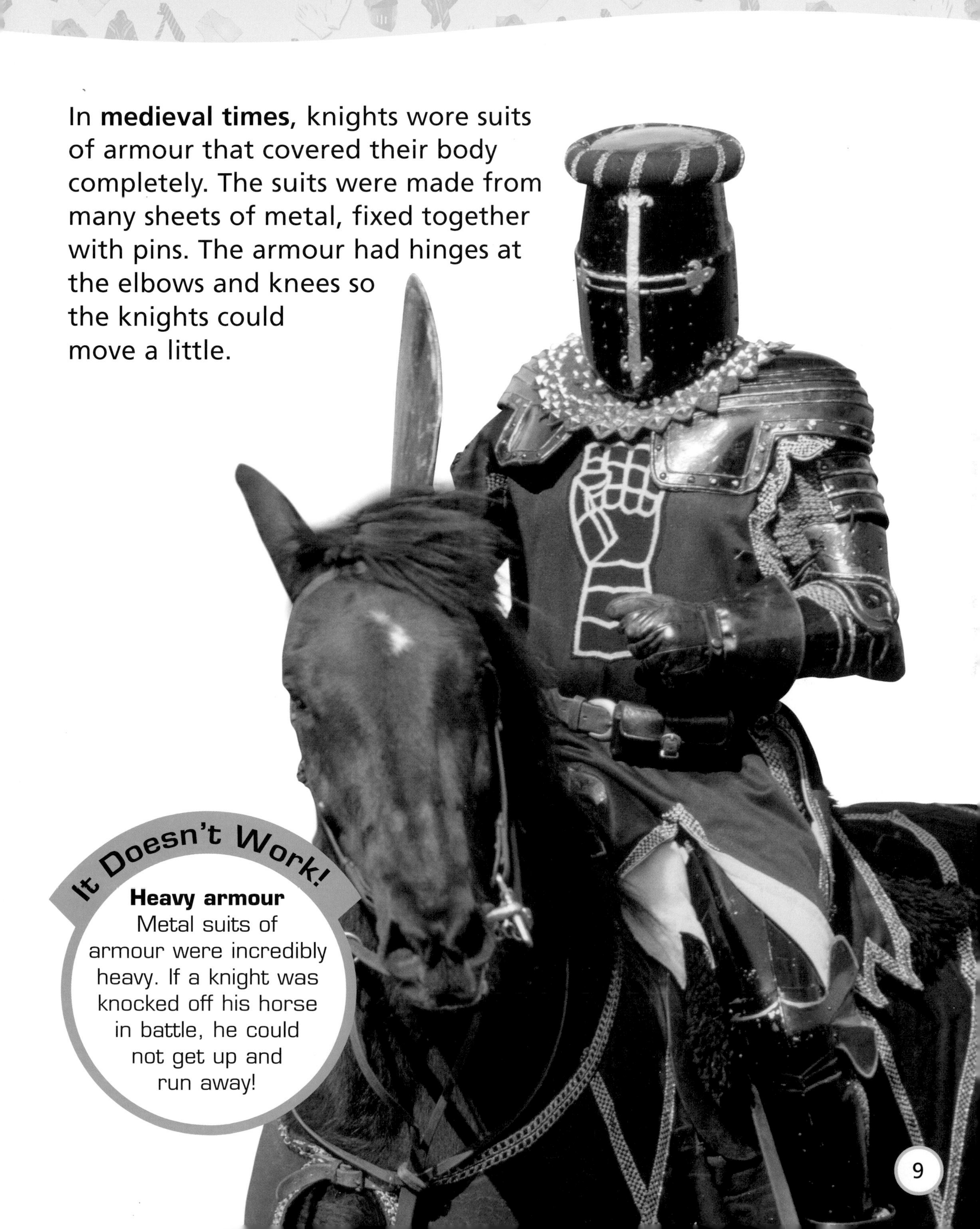

It Doesn't Work!

Heavy armour
Metal suits of armour were incredibly heavy. If a knight was knocked off his horse in battle, he could not get up and run away!

In the 1700s, many people in Europe worked on the land. Farmworkers dressed for work in a loose top, called a smock. Most farm workers wore wooden **clogs** that lasted for years.

By the 1850s, there were many cowboys working as cattle herders in America. Cowboys had a hat with a wide brim to keep the sun off their face. They wore trousers and shirts made from strong, tough cotton. They also protected their legs with leather over-trousers, known as **chaps**.

This painting shows a farmworker wearing a smock. His daughter wears a ***pinafore*** *over her dress.*

In the 1900s, all large houses had servants, and all the servants wore uniforms. Maids wore a black dress, with a white apron and cap. **Butlers** wore a black jacket, with two long tails at the back, and a waistcoat and striped trousers.

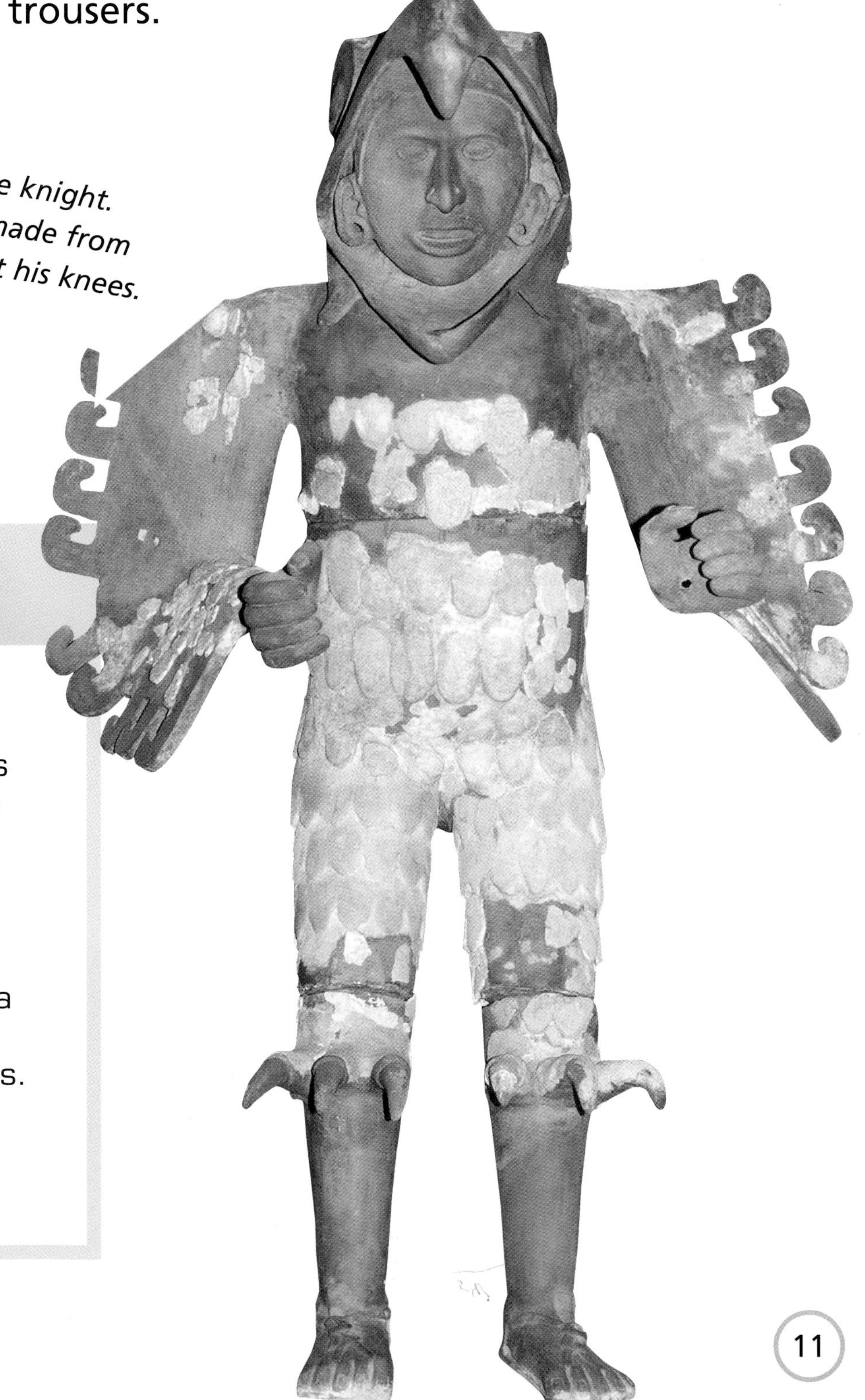

A clay model of an Aztec eagle knight. The knight wears a costume made from eagles' feathers, with claws at his knees.

Weird and Wonderful

Eagle knights

The Aztec people lived in Mexico around 600 years ago. Aztec warriors were fierce fighters, but the fiercest of all were the eagle knights.

Eagle knights dressed in a costume made from an eagle's feathers and claws. They even had an eagle's head fixed on to their helmet.

What are uniforms and workwear made from?

Uniforms and workwear are made from a wide range of materials, but strong, hardwearing fabrics are especially useful.

Cotton is often used for working clothes. It is comfortable to wear, and easy to wash. Some types of cotton, such as denim, are very hardwearing and good to wear for heavy, outdoor work.

Today, cotton is often mixed with **polyester**. The result is a lightweight fabric that does not crease easily.

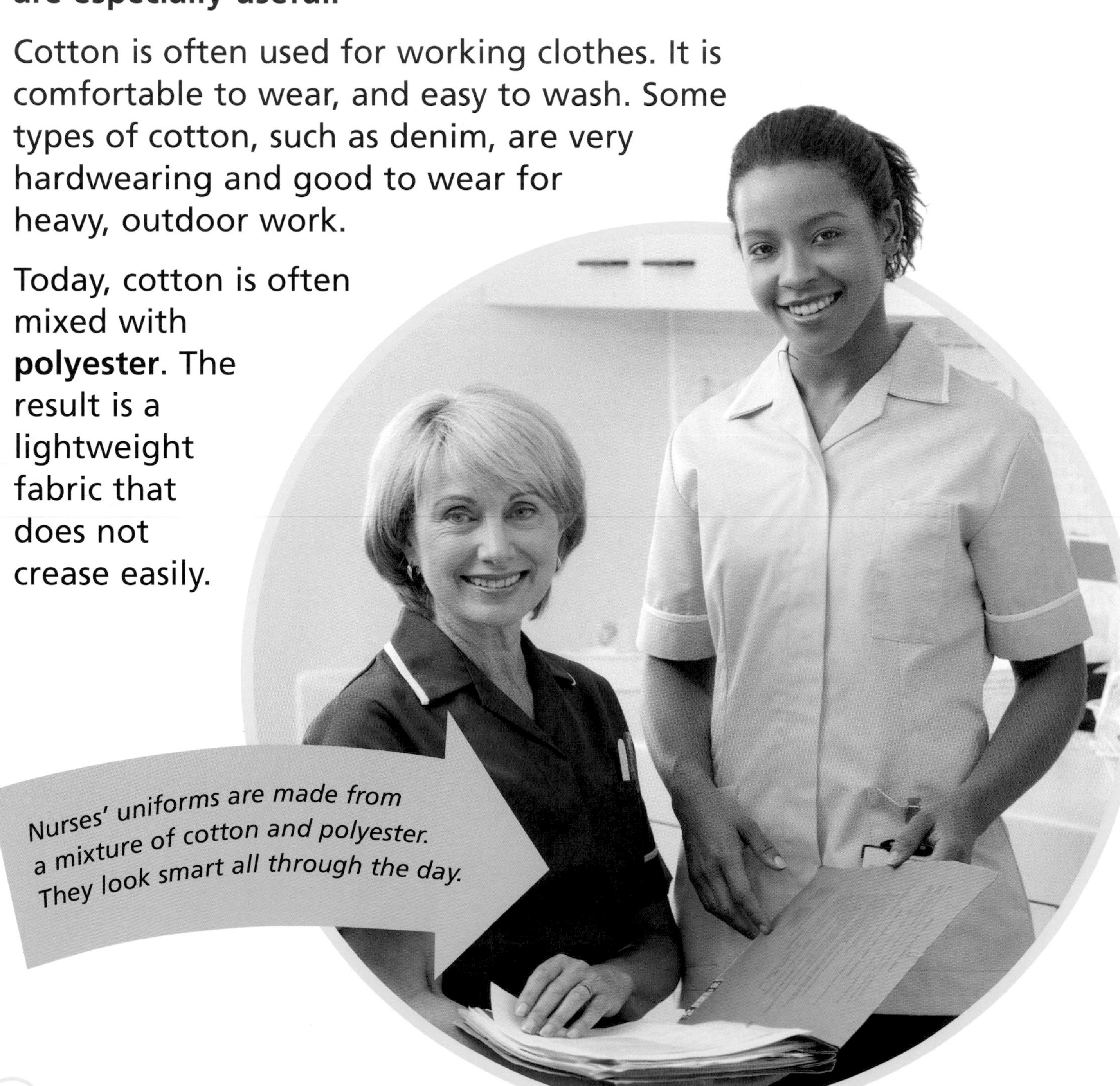

Nurses' uniforms are made from a mixture of cotton and polyester. They look smart all through the day.

Leather is a useful material for workwear because it is tough and **waterproof**. It is used to make strong work boots, gloves and belts. Work boots often have a metal toecap to protect the workers' toes.

Flashback

Denim jeans

The first denim jeans were made in California in the 1850s. A man called Levi Strauss made tough working trousers using denim. The trousers were worn by cowboys, and they soon became very popular. Now, people around the world wear denim clothes for leisure.

The cowboy on the left has leather chaps over his denim jeans.

Workmen wear thick leather boots and gloves, tough denim coveralls and plastic hardhats. **High-visibility** jackets make them easy to spot.

People who do dangerous work often wear a helmet to protect their head. These lightweight helmets, known as hardhats, are made from plastic.

Rubber is a very useful material for workwear because it can be moulded into any shape. Workers wear rubber boots to keep their feet dry and rubber gloves to protect their hands. Doctors and dentists wear gloves to prevent germs from spreading. Their gloves are made from a type of rubber known as latex. Latex gloves are very thin and **flexible** so that doctors and dentists can use their hands normally.

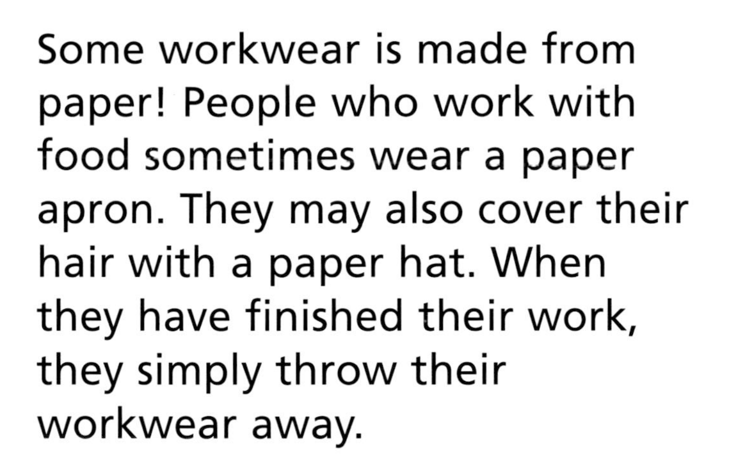

Some workwear is made from paper! People who work with food sometimes wear a paper apron. They may also cover their hair with a paper hat. When they have finished their work, they simply throw their workwear away.

What Would You Wear?

You need to cut a path through thick, scratchy bushes. What material would you choose for your work clothes?

A. Lightweight cotton
B. Wool
C. Paper
D. Denim

(Answer on p31)

This Japanese chef has a paper hat and wears a rubber glove to prepare the food.

Workwear and uniforms for protection and safety

When people do dangerous jobs they need clothes to keep them safe. Workers on building sites wear a plastic hardhat and heavy boots. Builders sometimes wear a safety harness round their waist. The harness is fixed to a safe place on the building.

Soldiers wear **camouflage** suits when they do not want to be seen. Camouflage is a patterned material that is specially designed to blend into the background.

These soldiers are all dressed in desert camouflage suits. The camouflage makes them harder to see in a sandy landscape.

Soldiers in the jungle wear camouflage suits in shades of dark green and brown. When they are in the desert, they wear paler camouflage.

For some workers, it is very important to be seen. People who work on roads or airport runways wear very bright clothes to make them easy to see. These brightly coloured clothes are known as high-visibility or hi-vis suits.

It Works!

Hi-vis clothes

Hi-vis clothes are made from material that reflects the light. During the day they look extremely bright. At night they reflect back any lights and shine in the dark.

It Doesn't Work!

Awkward eagles
In the past, American firefighters had a metal eagle's head on their helmet. It looked great, but the eagle sometimes got caught on windows and doors. Now most firefighters wear a plain helmet.

Firefighters are in great danger from flames and choking smoke. They also have to enter buildings that are very unsafe.

Firefighters wear fire-resistant suits and oxygen masks. Fire-resistant suits are made from material that is very hard to set on fire. Oxygen masks allow people to breathe normally, even when a building is full of smoke. The mask also covers the firefighters' eyes, so they are protected from burning smoke.

When they enter a burning building, firefighters wear helmets and boots. Their helmets protect their heads from falling objects. Their boots have heat-proof soles, so they can walk on surfaces that are burning hot.

Sometimes firefighters have to enter a place where there are dangerous ***chemicals****. They need special suits and masks to protect them from the burning chemicals.*

All sorts of workwear

People wear all sorts of clothes for work. Ballet dancers, gymnasts and clowns all have special costumes. Footballers, tennis players and cyclists wear different kinds of sportswear, and businessmen and women usually dress in suits.

Chefs often wear a white hat, with a white tunic and trousers. Many waiters and waitresses dress in black and white. Waiters in smart restaurants wear a black suit, with a white shirt and a black bow-tie.

Waiters and waitresses usually look smart and clean. This makes people confident about eating in their restaurant.

In some countries, **lawyers** dress in special clothes to appear in court. They wear a long black robe with a curly wig on their head. Religious leaders, monks and nuns also wear special clothes. The clothes are a sign of their religion and they make them very easy to recognize.

Buddhist monks wear simple robes dyed yellow or orange.

Weird and Wonderful

High shoes for chefs
In the past, chefs in Japan wore very high sandals. The sandals had wooden soles that stood on two wooden blocks. These raised sandals kept the chef's clothes well away from the kitchen floor. Some chef's sandals stood on blocks that were 16cm (6 inches) high!

Divers and astronauts need special suits to keep them alive under the ocean or out in space.

Deep-sea divers wear a thick rubber suit. They have a mask covering their face and they carry an oxygen tank on their back. A tube from the tank leads to the mask, so they can breathe underwater. Divers have a knife strapped to their leg in case they get trapped and need to cut their way out of trouble.

It Works!

Fantastic flippers

Deep-sea divers have long rubber flippers strapped to their feet. When the divers kick their feet, they move very fast through the water. Wearing flippers makes a diver swim more like a fish!

Astronauts cannot survive in space without special clothing. They have to wear a spacesuit that covers them completely. Astronauts also wear a large space helmet that is connected to an oxygen tank. The helmet has a radio microphone and speakers, so astronauts can talk to one another.

Spacesuits are made up of many layers. The inner layer is cooled by liquid to keep the astronaut's body at the right temperature.

All sorts of uniforms

When people wear a uniform, it makes them easy to spot in a crowd. People who work on buses, trains or planes all wear a special outfit, so you can find them quickly if you need help.

All over the world, the police wear uniforms that are easy to spot. Most police officers wear a large peaked cap that makes them stand out and a uniform that shows they are in the police force.

This police officer works in New York. His uniform is hardwearing and easy to recognize.

Wearing a uniform shows that you belong to a special group or organization. The organization may be a company, a school, or even a brass band. When people wear a uniform, it helps them to feel part of their organization.

It Works!

Red Cross workers

The International Red Cross is an organization that helps people in need. All Red Cross members wear the same sign – a large red cross on a white background. People everywhere recognize the sign. They know that the Red Cross workers are there to help them.

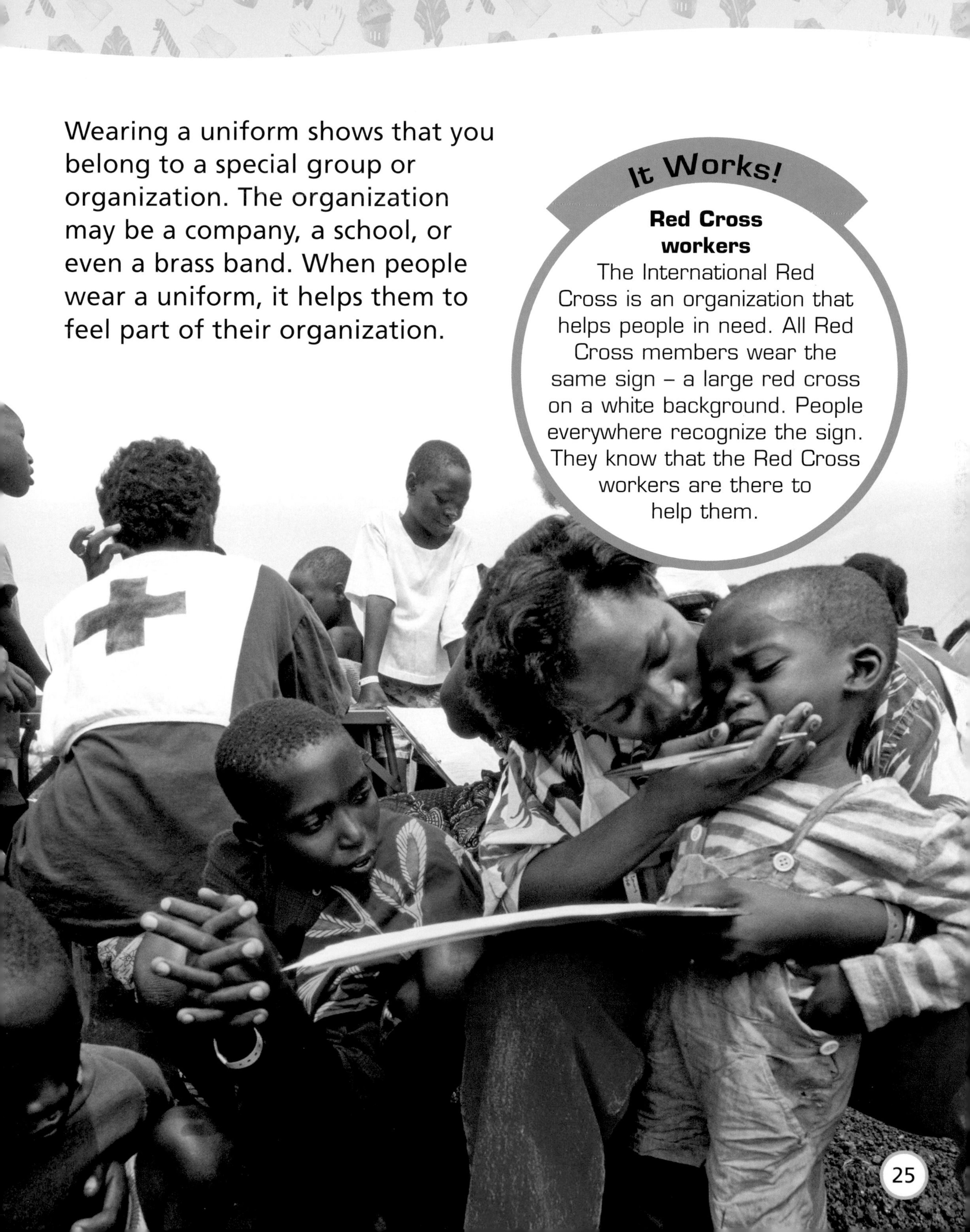

Members of the **armed services**, such as soldiers and sailors, all have uniforms. Before they march in a parade, they have an inspection to make sure that their uniforms are looking really good.

Adults are not the only people who wear uniforms. Many children wear uniforms for school. Some youth organizations also have a uniform. Scouts and guides all over the world wear a similar outfit.

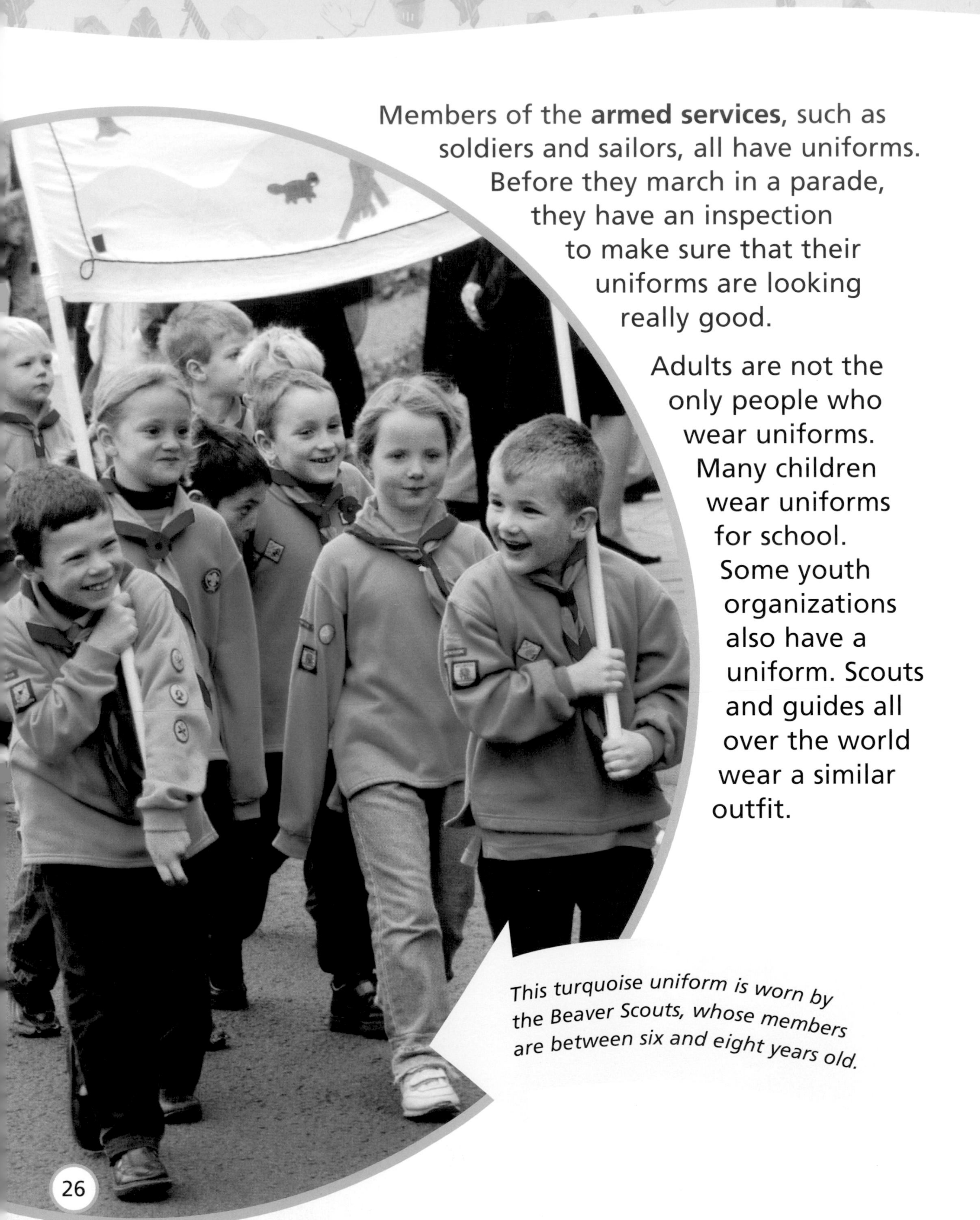

This turquoise uniform is worn by the Beaver Scouts, whose members are between six and eight years old.

In a few schools, pupils wear very fancy uniforms. But most school uniforms are quite simple. For example, in some schools all the pupils wear a red top and black trousers.

Next time you walk down a busy street, take a good look around you. How many different work clothes and uniforms can you see?

Flashback

Sailor tops

In the past, sailors wore a blue and white top with a very wide collar. Now, sailors wear modern uniforms, but sailor-style clothes are still popular. Schoolgirls in Japan often wear a sailor top as a part of their school uniform!

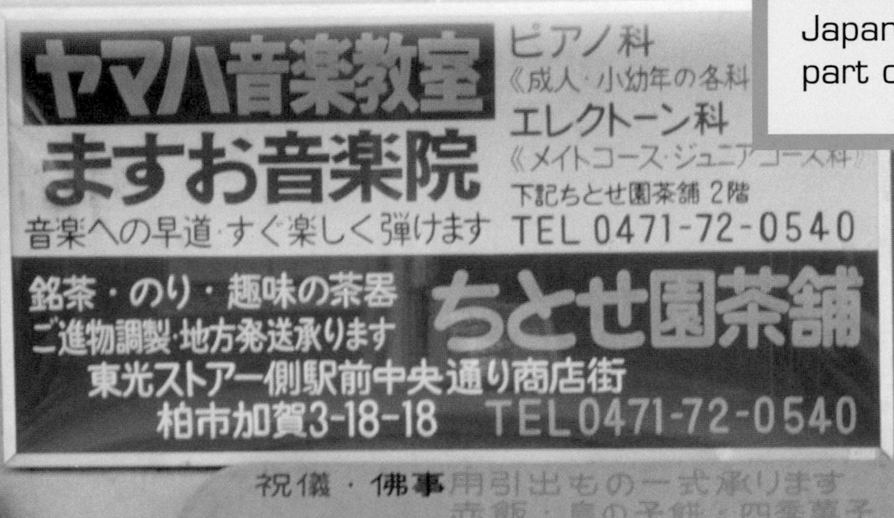

Make your own space helmet

This space helmet will take you three days to make because it needs to dry out at each stage. It is made from a balloon covered with papier-maché.

You will need:

* a large balloon
* a heavy pot
* a large bowl of papier-maché (made from long strips of newspaper mixed with PVA glue and water)
* paint and paintbrush
* thick tape
* piece of tubing

Figure 1

1. Blow up the balloon and stand it in the pot. Cover the balloon with two layers of papier-maché.

Figure 2

2. Leave the balloon standing in the pot overnight. Next day, add two more layers of papier-maché and let the balloon dry overnight.

Figure 3

3. Pop the balloon and remove it. Ask an adult to cut around the helmet base, and cut a hole in the side for the face area.

Figure 4

4. Tape around the cut edges to make your helmet stronger. Paint your helmet, adding any details you like.

You could add a breathing tube, as in this picture, to make your helmet more realistic.

Dress-up box

5-minute French chef

French chefs often wear a white hat, with a white top and trousers. Sometimes they wear a striped apron and a colourful scarf.

To create your costume, you will need an apron, and a thick tea-towel for your hat. You will also need a large sock to fix your hat in place. If you add a red neckscarf, you will look very French.

1. Fold the tea-towel in half and wind it round your head.
2. Ask an adult to tie the sock tightly round your forehead. This will hold the hat firmly in place.
3. Put on your apron and your neckscarf. Now grab a wooden spoon and bowl and get ready to cook!

Glossary

armed services – the army, navy and airforce, and all the other organizations that fight in times of war

Buddhist – someone who follows the teaching of the Lord Buddha. The religion of Buddhism is practised mainly in Asia.

butler – a senior male servant, who often welcomes guests to a house

camouflage – clothing that makes people blend into their surroundings

chaps – tough leg coverings that are worn over trousers, especially by cattle herders

chemicals – substances, such as acid, that are often used in factories. Some chemicals are poisonous or can cause very serious burns.

clogs – heavy wooden shoes with a low back and a painted, turned-up toe

flexible – able to bend easily

high-visibility – very bright and easy to see

Inuit – a race of people who live in the Arctic regions

lawyer – someone who gives advice to people about their rights, and speaks for them in court

medieval times – a period of history between the years 1000 and 1450

organization – a large company, or a large group of people who all work together

pinafore – a kind of dress that women and girls wear over their clothes to keep them clean. Pinafores are usually sleeveless.

polyester – a substance made in a factory that is used to make a hard-wearing fabric and a type of plastic

rank – a job level in an organization, such as the army

waterproof – when an item of clothing is waterproof, it does not allow water to pass through it

What would you wear?

Answer to the question on page 15.

The best choice for your work clothes is D. Denim is very tough so it will protect you from scratchy bushes. Lightweight cotton will not give you enough protection. Wool gets caught on bushes and paper gets torn!

Index

Photos or pictures are shown below in bold, **like this**.